A——

Dad and I picked [this] book in Tucson while visiting Kristie and Mark. I really like some of these recipes so I hope you will try them and remember that we love sharing our own recipes as well.

With Love,

Mom

Tacos

Susan Curtis and Daniel Hoyer
with R. Allen Smith

Photography by
Lois Ellen Frank

GIBBS·SMITH
P
PUBLISHER

SALT LAKE CITY

This series of cookbooks is dedicated to the friends and guests of the Santa Fe School of Cooking, whose loyal support and patronage helped the school achieve success beyond anyone's wildest dreams.

First Edition
04 03 02 01 00   5 4 3 2 1

Text © 2000 by Susan D. Curtis and the Santa Fe School of Cooking
Photographs © 2000 by Lois Ellen Frank
      (LOIS Photography, Santa Fe, New Mexico, [505] 466-6306)

Published by
Gibbs Smith, Publisher
P.O. Box 667
Layton, Utah 84041

Orders: (800) 748-5439
Web site: www.gibbs-smith.com

Edited by Linda Nimori
Designed and produced by FORTHGEAR, Inc.
Printed in Hong Kong

Library of Congress Cataloging-in-Publication Data

Curtis, Susan, 1946–
      Tacos / Susan Curtis and Daniel Hoyer, with R. Allen Smith ; photography by Lois Ellen Frank.— 1st ed.
            p. cm. — (The Santa Fe School of Cooking series)
      Includes index.
      ISBN 0-87905-947-8
      1. Tacos. I. Hoyer, Daniel. II. Smith, R. Allen, 1953– III. Title IV. Series.

TX836 C.87 2000
641.8—dc21
                                                                                    00-035757

CONTENTS

◎ INTRODUCTION ◎

What are tacos? Mention tacos and you may conjure up images of crispy fried corn tortillas filled with ground beef and garnished with lettuce, tomato, and shredded yellow cheese—Webster's definition; or you might think of a colorful, stand-up street stall in Mexico with tacos of handmade soft tortillas topped with carne asada or carnitas, guacamole, and salsa. Both examples are genuine tacos, as is also a late-night snack of meats and sauces left over from a large meal, or *comida*, and wrapped in tortillas. There is no right or wrong when it comes to tacos, only different ideas. At the Santa Fe School of Cooking, we define a taco as any tasty filling served in or on flour or corn tortillas, whether crispy or soft.

While the use of chiles is important for the flavor of many taco recipes, that does not mean that you have to like your food hot to enjoy tacos. Although chiles can provide that searing, sweat-producing heat that many of us enjoy, the flavor of chiles is much more important than the heat. In Mexico, where the chile is revered, the flavors are more subtle than incendiary, and salsas and chiles are served on the side to allow each individual to customize the piquancy. These recipes have been constructed to allow the enjoyment of chile flavor without forcing a tongue-numbing experience on unsuspecting eaters, but it is important for the cook to taste while preparing food with chiles. There are relative heat scales for most chiles, but climate and growing conditions can greatly vary the intensity of chiles. In fact, two chiles from the same plant often have quite different levels of heat.

One thing is certain: Tacos are fun! What better way to liven up a get-together of family or friends than to serve up a selection of scrumptious fillings along with a variety of salsas and condiments so that everyone can create their own customized meal? This book contains recipes ranging from traditional to contemporary, chosen to help illustrate the limitless possibilities for preparing tacos. We are certain that you will enjoy our selections and encourage you to use your own creativity to develop variations and new ideas.

PIPERADE BRUNCH TACOS

These tacos have their origin in the Basque egg dish called *Piperade*. Simple and easy to prepare, this filling adapts well to variations, so use your creativity. Serve them as a simple breakfast or as part of an elaborate feast.

Yield: 16 to 18 tacos, 8 servings

Taco Filling

1 medium onion, diced

3 tablespoons butter or olive oil

1 red pepper, diced, or a combination of red pepper and poblano or jalapeño chiles (may also be roasted and peeled before dicing)

1 clove garlic, peeled and minced

2 ripe tomatoes, cored and diced

1 teaspoon dried Mexican oregano, or 2 teaspoons chopped fresh herbs (like thyme or marjoram)

12 to 16 ounces chorizo, sliced or diced (a lightly cured, shaped sausage is best for this), or substitute smoked sausage or ham

8 large eggs, well beaten with salt and pepper

Grated cheese (optional)

Chile caribe (optional)

Tacos

Flour or corn tortillas

1. Saute onion in butter until golden in color. Add peppers and garlic; cook for 2 additional minutes.

2. Add tomato and oregano; cook 3 to 5 minutes more to evaporate most of the liquid.

3. Place chorizo in pan; saute for 2 to 3 minutes to heat and to release the fat.

4. Add beaten eggs and cook, stirring and scraping occasionally, to desired doneness.

5. Turn onto a warmed serving dish or platter and top with grated cheese and chile caribe if desired. Roll or fold in warm, homemade flour or corn tortillas.

Serving suggestion: Great with sauteed potatoes, fresh fruit, and red and green salsas.

ADOBO PORK TACOS WITH GRILLED PINEAPPLE

Chef Daniel Hoyer fondly remembers eating these tacos on a hot October afternoon in Tequila, Mexico. He claims them in his "top ten" taco experiences. Maybe the tequila and the ice-cold cerveza helped too.

Yield: enough for 24 tacos

Taco Filling

4 pounds boneless, trimmed pork loin, cut in half-inch slices
1 medium white onion, chopped
2 ancho and 2 guajillo chiles, toasted, stemmed, and seeded
1 tablespoon puree of chipotle chiles in adobo
6 cloves garlic
1-1/2 ounces achiote paste
1/8 cup apple cider vinegar or rice wine vinegar
2 teaspoons honey
1/4 cup chopped fresh cilantro

1 tablespoon vegetable oil
4 cloves
1/4 cup water
1 teaspoon salt
1/2 teaspoon freshly ground black pepper
1 fresh ripe pineapple, peeled, cored, and cut lengthwise in half-inch-thick slices, then lightly brushed with vegetable oil

Tacos

Corn tortillas

1. Arrange slices of pork on a cutting board or smooth countertop between layers of plastic wrap. Using a meat-tenderizing mallet or a rolling pin, flatten the slices to form sheets about a quarter inch thick.

2. Place chiles, onion, garlic, achiote, vinegar, honey, cilantro, oil, water, cloves, salt, and pepper in a blender and puree smooth.

3. Spread mixture evenly over the sheets of pork and marinate in refrigerator for 1 to 3 hours. Remove from refrigerator 1/2 hour before cooking.

4. Preheat a charcoal or gas grill or oven broiler to produce a medium-high heat.

5. Place pineapple slices on grill alongside the marinated pork. Cook about 3 to 4 minutes on one side and turn over. Continue cooking until slightly charred and cooked through.

6. Remove from heat, cover and allow to rest for 5 to 10 minutes. Cut pork in quarter-inch strips. Garnish: pineapple may be sliced small as well or served in large slices.

7. Arrange on soft corn tortillas and top with garnishes.

Serving suggestion: Serve with refried beans, Mexican rice, and an assortment of condiments such as roasted jalapeño chiles, Roasted Tomatillo Salsa (see Salsas, p. 7), Mexican cheese, avocados, grilled onions, lime, and toasted oregano.

PORK CARNITAS TACOS

Carnitas, or "little meats," are very popular in Mexico and can be found in many parts of the United States as well. Many restaurants in Mexico feature carnitas on the weekends. Good carnitas are usually an indicator of an establishment's overall food quality. The traditional method of preparation can be an all-day process, but we have developed an approach that works well and is much easier. This recipe divulges a "secret" ingredient that many cooks use—Coca-Cola™—and we know of no substitute. If you don't have any or would rather not use it, simply replace the Coke™ with water; however, the carnitas will not brown as well.

Yield: about 24 tacos

Taco Filling
2 to 2-1/2 pounds pork stew meat or trimmed pork butt, cut into 1-inch cubes
4 ounces lard
1 teaspoon coarse salt
1 ancho chile, toasted, stems and seeds removed, and ground to powder (1-1/2 tablespoons)
1 guajillo or New Mexico red chile, toasted, stems and seeds removed, and ground to powder (1-1/2 tablespoons)

1 teaspoon ground, toasted cumin seed
6 whole allspice
3 whole cloves
6 cloves of garlic, peeled
2 bay leaves
1 cup Coca-Cola™ (not Diet Coke™)
2-1/2 cups meat broth or water
1 whole orange
Tacos
Flour or corn tortillas

1. Heat lard in a heavy saucepan until hot. (Don't use a pan that is too broad; a 10- or 12-inch bottom will keep the ingredients from spreading too far.)

2. Toss pork pieces with salt, ground chiles, and cumin seed. Cook in lard for 8 to 10 minutes, turning frequently to evenly brown.

3. Add allspice, cloves, garlic, and bay leaves, then the Coke™, broth or water, and whole orange.

4. Bring to a full boil, then reduce heat to just boiling. Cook, stirring occasionally, until most of the liquid has been absorbed and the lard is beginning to sizzle, about 1-1/4 hours. (The meat should be fork tender; if not, add more water and continue cooking).

5. Remove orange, turn heat up to medium high, and saute meat while stirring until pieces are well browned with caramelized edges. Remove from pan and drain well.

6. Serve with assorted condiments and fresh tortillas for build-your-own tacos. Carnitas are especially good with avocado or Guacamole (see p. 36).

TACOS AL PASTOR

Tacos al Pastor, literally "shepherd's tacos," are filled with hearty stew-like meat. This is an adaptation from one of Santa Fe's favorite authentic Mexican restaurants, the Old Mexico Grill. Commercially in Mexico, the meat is cooked on a rotating spit and carved into thin slices to fill tacos, but we like this home-style approach created by this restaurant.

Yield: 20 to 24 tacos, 8 to 10 servings

Taco Filling

4 ounces (about 8) dry ancho chiles, stemmed and seeded
2 cups water
3 to 4 roasted plum tomatoes, coarsely chopped,
    or 3/4 cup chopped canned tomatoes
2 tablespoons vegetable oil
3 pounds pork stew meat, trimmed and cubed pork butt,
    or cubed pork cushion meat
1/2 cup finely diced white onion
8 cloves of garlic, peeled and minced
1 tablespoon toasted dried Mexican oregano

1 teaspoon lightly toasted, ground cumin seed
1 teaspoon chopped fresh or dry thyme leaves (optional)
4 whole bay leaves
1 teaspoon freshly ground black pepper
1/8 cup apple cider vinegar or unseasoned
    rice wine vinegar
3/4 cup pineapple juice
2 teaspoons granulated sugar
1 teaspoon salt

Tacos

Corn tortillas

1. Toast chiles on a skillet or comal or in a hot oven (425 degrees) until darkened slightly but not burned.

2. Bring water to a boil, add toasted chiles, stir well and remove from heat. Soak chiles for 15 to 20 minutes, drain and reserve water. Puree chiles in a blender with a little of the water and the tomatoes.

3. Heat oil in a 4- to 5-quart saucepan or in a pressure cooker. Brown meat a little at a time, remove, and reserve cooked pieces.

4. Add onions and then garlic and cook until onion is softened and begins to brown, about 2 minutes. Add oregano, cumin, thyme, bay leaves, and pepper along with chile-tomato puree and fry for one additional minute, stirring constantly.

5. Return browned pork to the pan and add vinegar, pineapple juice, sugar, salt, and 1 cup of reserved chile soaking water.

6. Bring to a boil, reduce heat, cover and cook for 35 minutes at 15 pounds in the pressure cooker. (Note: If using a regular pan, cook covered on low heat for about 1-1/2 hours until meat is tender. You may need to add water during the cooking process to prevent burning.)

7. Strain the sauce from the meat and cook longer, if needed, to thicken.

8. To serve, shred meat and place in soft corn tortillas. Garnish with chopped green onions and serve with Guacamole (see p. 36), some of the reserved sauce, Salsa Fresca (see p. 37), and lime wedges.

COCHINITA PIBIL

Pibil is the Mayan word for the pit that is dug then lined with stones to roast a suckling pig. A fire is built and allowed to burn for several hours until it has been reduced to smoldering coals. Meanwhile, the *cochinita*, or little pig, has been seasoned and marinated with the exotic flavors of the brick-red achiote, the bright taste of citrus, and the floral heat of the habanero chile. Wrapped in banana leaves, the meat is placed in the pit, covered with the rocks and some palm leaves, and slow roasted overnight. This feast is then served family style with fresh handmade tortillas, salsas, condiments, and salads to make your own tacos.

Cochinita Pibil is a festive meal, excellent for parties and gatherings; the long, unattended cooking period allows time in the kitchen for the preparation of salsas, condiments, and side dishes. This recipe has been developed to provide the home cook with a close and quite good alternative to pit cooking. We have also had success with using the combination of a backyard smoker for 1-1/2 hours and the remainder of the time in the house oven. Although the banana leaves lend a distinct flavor to the meat as well as a dramatic presentation, a package of aluminum foil instead of leaves also produces an outstanding dish.

Yield: about 3-1/2 pounds cooked meat, enough for 30 to 36 tacos

Taco Filling

1 medium, boneless pork butt (4 to 6 pounds), trimmed but with some fat remaining
3 ounces achiote paste
12 cloves peeled garlic
1 medium white onion, coarsely chopped (3/4 cup)
10 cracked allspice berries, or 2 teaspoons ground allspice
2 tablespoons toasted dried Mexican oregano
1 teaspoon toasted cumin seed
2 teaspoons cracked black pepper
6 bay leaves
2 tablespoons Worcestershire sauce
Juice of 2 limes
Juice of 1 orange
1/4 cup apple cider vinegar or rice wine vinegar
2 fresh habanero or Scotch bonnet chiles, stems and seeds removed, or 2 tablespoons bottled habanero chile sauce
2 tablespoons vegetable oil
1 teaspoon salt
1 package (1 pound) frozen banana leaves (available at specialty food stores and Latin American or Asian grocers). Thaw and rinse well in cool water. Tear 8 half-inch-wide strips off one leaf and tie two together to make four strips.

Tacos

Corn tortillas

(continued on page 8)

COCHINITA PIBIL

(continued from page 6)

1. Place pork in a freezer bag or other large plastic bag.

2. Mix all other ingredients except banana leaves in a blender or food processor. Pour in with pork, seal bag, and distribute well to coat meat. Marinate at least 2 hours or overnight in refrigerator.

3. Preheat oven to 325 degrees.

4. Line the bottom of a heavy roasting pan with 2 or 3 banana leaves. They should overlap the pan on all sides.

5. Remove pork roast from the bag and reserve marinade.

6. Place pork fat-side-up on banana leaves in the pan. Pour about 1/2 cup of marinade over top of meat.

7. Place 3 or 4 more leaves over pork and inside bottom leaves. Pull bottom leaves around meat; tie strips of banana leaves around this package from both directions to secure.

8. Bake at 325 degrees for 3-1/2 to 4 hours until meat is tender. Leaves may be almost black on the outside when finished.

9. Allow to cool for 20 minutes; then slit open banana leaves with a sharp knife or scissors (be careful of the steam) and remove pork.

Serving suggestion: Fresh Corn Tortillas (see p. 31), habanero salsa, Pickled Red Onions (see p. 35), sliced radishes, chopped cilantro, citrus wedges, Guacamole (see p. 36), and jicama salad.

TACOS OF CALABACITAS

On the street in Mexico, these tacos are sometimes called *Entomates*, referring to the way the tortillas are dipped in a simmered tomato and chile sauce before they are cooked on the comal or griddle. Although they are tacos, they could also be described as enchiladas.

Calabacitas are prepared throughout the Southwest as well as in Mexico and are simply cut-up "little squash," generally summer varieties. Traditional preparations are varied, but this typical recipe features a combination of the squash and fire-roasted corn cooked with chiles and garlic.

Yield: about 24 tacos

Sauce:

2 tablespoons vegetable oil
1/2 cup diced white onion
6 cloves garlic, peeled
2 teaspoons toasted dried Mexican oregano
1 ancho chile, dry-toasted in a heavy skillet until barely charred, stems and seeds removed, and crumbled, or 1 tablespoon toasted ancho chile powder

1 guajillo or New Mexican red chile, dry-toasted in a heavy skillet until barely charred, stems and seeds removed, and crumbled, or 1 tablespoon toasted New Mexican chile powder
8 plum tomatoes, stem core removed, roasted on a Santa Fe Grill (see p. 39) or under a broiler until slightly blackened
1 teaspoon toasted ground cumin seed
1/2 to 3/4 cup water
Salt to taste

1. Preheat a heavy skillet or pan to medium heat and add oil. Add onion and garlic cloves; gently saute until onions are translucent and garlic is beginning to brown. Increase heat to high and add oregano, chiles, tomatoes, and cumin; fry for 1 minute more.

2. Add 1/2 cup of water and reduce heat to simmer.

3. Allow to cook for 15 minutes and place in a blender, adding more water if needed. Puree to a smooth consistency.

4. Return to pan and simmer for 30 minutes longer, adding more liquid as needed to prevent burning (finished sauce should be about as thick as good spaghetti sauce). Adjust for salt.

(continued on next page)

TACOS OF CALABACITAS

(continued from previous page)

Taco Filling
2 tablespoons butter or vegetable oil
1 teaspoon salt
2 zucchini squash, diced 3/8- to 1/2-inch square
(about 1-1/2 cups diced)
2 yellow summer or crookneck squash, diced 3/8-
to 1/2-inch square (about 1-1/2 cups diced)
5 cloves garlic, peeled and thinly sliced
1 teaspoon chopped fresh marjoram or toasted dried
Mexican oregano

1/2 cup New Mexican green, Anaheim, or poblano
chile, flame-roasted on a Santa Fe Grill (see p. 39)
or under a broiler and peeled,
or use chopped frozen New Mexican green chiles
1 cup roasted corn kernels or frozen corn kernels
1/2 cup water
Pepper to taste
Tacos
24 to 28 fresh corn tortillas
8 ounces asadero or Monterey jack cheese, grated

1. Preheat a heavy saute pan or skillet to medium hot (325 to 345 degrees). Add oil or butter or a combination of the two.

2. Add squash and salt; cook, stirring often, for about 1 minute.

3. Add garlic and marjoram; cook for about 2 minutes more.

4. Add chiles, corn, water, and black pepper; continue cooking and stirring until most of the liquid has evaporated. Set aside until ready to assemble tacos.

When all ingredients are prepared, preheat a comal, griddle, or large skillet to medium hot (325 to 345 degrees). Brush the griddle with a light coating of vegetable oil, then dip a tortilla in the tomato sauce and place the tortilla on the comal. Place some calabacitas and 1/3 ounce of the cheese on the tortilla; fold in half. Cook on one side for about 1 minute, turn over, and continue cooking for 1 minute more. Repeat with remaining tacos. Serve immediately or reheat in a 350-degree oven. The leftover sauce may be poured over the tacos for garnish.

Serving suggestions: This is excellent as a side dish with roasted chicken or as a buffet course.

HOT AND SMOKY SHRIMP TACOS

The flavor and the spiciness of chipotle chiles, which are smoked red jalapeños, make a perfect foil for the garlicky shrimp. This dish was meant to be hot, but you can vary the intensity of heat by reducing the quantity of chile. If you like, the shrimp may also be prepared using an outdoor grill; make the sauce without the shrimp, then brush some on the shrimp before grilling. Toss shrimp with the remaining sauce after they are cooked.

Yield: 20 to 25 tacos, 8 to 10 servings

Taco Filling
3 tablespoons olive oil
1 tablespoon butter
8 cloves garlic, sliced
1-1/2 pounds medium shrimp (26 to 30 per pound), peeled and deveined
1-1/2 teaspoons coarse salt
1/8 to 1/4 cup (some like it hot!) pureed chipotle chiles in adobo

1/2 cup roasted tomato puree or canned tomato sauce
2 tablespoons cold water
Juice of 1/2 orange
Juice of 1 lime
1/2 cup chopped cilantro (about 1/2 large bunch)
Tacos
Fresh corn tortillas

1. Preheat a heavy skillet or saute pan to medium hot (325 degrees); add olive oil and butter and continue heating until oil begins to smoke (400 degrees). Immediately add garlic, shrimp, and salt, stirring or tossing vigorously. Oil tends to splatter at this temperture, so be careful.

2. When shrimp begin to turn opaque, stir in the chipotle chile puree and saute about 15 seconds to completely coat shrimp.

3. Add tomato puree, water, and orange and lime juices.

4. Reduce heat slightly and bring to a boil for 1 minute. Remove from heat and stir in cilantro.

5. Serve in fresh soft corn tortillas, 2 or 3 shrimp per taco.

Serving suggestion: Garnish tacos with shredded romaine lettuce, Salsa Verde (see p. 37), sliced avocados, radishes, lime wedges, and a dollop of sour cream. Serve with white rice and black beans.

CHARGRILLED FISH TACOS
WITH CARIBBEAN SEASONINGS

On the island of Cozumel and throughout the Yucatan, achiote is a favorite seasoning for fresh fish. We have combined it with other exciting tropical flavors for a seasoning rub for fish tacos. This seasoning also works great for shrimp, chicken, and turkey. The chargrill adds a hint of smoke, but this dish can be prepared in the oven or saute pan also.

Yield: 18 tacos, 6 to 8 servings

Taco Filling

3 to 3-1/2 pounds red snapper filets (or other firm-fleshed fish: red rockfish, tuna, mahi-mahi, sea bass), preferably fresh
2 ounces achiote paste
4 cloves garlic
Juice and zest of 1 lime
All of the juice and half of the zest of 1 orange
6 allspice berries, or 1-1/2 teaspoons ground allspice
1/2 teaspoon freshly ground black pepper
1 teaspoon coarse salt
4 tablespoons fresh cilantro leaves
1 fresh habanero chile, stemmed and seeded, or 1 tablespoon bottled habanero sauce
1 tablespoon apple cider vinegar or rice wine vinegar
1 tablespoon honey
2 tablespoons vegetable oil
1 tablespoon water

Tacos

Corn or flour tortillas

1. Place all filling ingredients except fish in a blender and puree smooth.

2. Evenly coat the fish filets with achiote mixture; cover and allow to marinate at room temperature for 20 to 30 minutes.

3. Cook fish on a charcoal or gas grill or in the oven broiler for approximately 3 minutes per side, depending on thickness of filets. (We think fish tastes best when cooked medium rare to medium, especially when it is very fresh.)

4. Allow to cool for a few minutes and slice for tacos.

5. Serve in soft corn or flour tortillas.

Serving suggestions: Garnish with a fresh fruit or tomato-habanero salsa or Pickled Red Onions (see p. 35) and lime wedges.

BAJA-STYLE FISH TACOS WITH CHIPOTLE MAYONNAISE

Rubio's Baja Grill in San Diego started the fish taco craze north of the border in 1983 when Ralph Rubio transplanted his favorite recipe from a small taco vendor on the Baja coast to his southern California restaurant. We are sharing our version of this beachside treat.

Yield: 16 generous tacos

Taco Filling

1-1/2 pounds cod filets (or other firm white fish),
**   cut in 2-1/2- by 1/2-inch pieces**
8 ounces full-flavored pale ale or Mexican lager
3 whole eggs, well beaten
2 teaspoons Coleman's dry mustard
1 tablespoon New Mexican or other red chile powder
1 tablespoon salt
2 teaspoons sugar
1-1/2 cups all-purpose flour + 1 cup for dredging
Oil for frying (preferably canola or peanut oil)

Tacos

Flour tortillas

1. Mix half of the beer with all other ingredients except fish and blend well with a whisk.

2. When all lumps have been smoothed, continue adding beer until a slightly thinner-than-pancake-batter consistency is attained. Keep chilled at all times.

3. Dredge fish filets in flour and dip in batter, being careful to completely coat. Allow excess to drip off.

4. Fry in 350-degree oil for 2-1/2 to 4 minutes, until golden brown and cooked through.

5. Drain well and allow to cool slightly.

6. When ready to serve, heat flour tortillas and place in a towel or cloth to keep warm. Re-fry the fish for about 1 more minute to make it crispy.

7. Spread tortillas with a tablespoon of Chipotle Mayonnaise (see below); add Spicy Coleslaw (see p. 34) or shredded lettuce, several pieces of fish, and guacamole or salsa if desired.

Chipotle Mayonnaise

1 cup mayonnaise
Juice of 1 lime
1 tablespoon chopped cilantro
1/8 teaspoon salt
1 tablespoon pureed chipotle chiles in adobo

1. Mix all ingredients well and refrigerate.

Note: this recipe is pictured on the front cover.

POLLO IN SALSA VERDE

Salsa Verde is a classic Mexican sauce that complements leftover cooked chicken and turkey, and also works well with sauteed shrimp or scallops. The lemony tartness of the tomatillos is balanced by the natural sweetness of the cooked garlic and onions with a little help from the sugar.

Yield: 20 to 24 tacos, 8 to 10 servings

Taco Filling
3/4 pound fresh tomatillos (about 8), husked and rinsed
    under hot tap water for 30 seconds
3 tablespoons vegetable oil
1/2 white onion, chopped
1 or 2 fresh jalapeño chiles, stems removed and sliced
4 cloves garlic, peeled
1/2 teaspoon salt
1 teaspoon granulated sugar
2 teaspoons chopped fresh epazote or marjoram,
    or 1 teaspoon toasted dried Mexican oregano

1 teaspoon apple cider vinegar or rice wine vinegar
1/2 cup water
2 or 3 chiles de arbol or other small dry red chiles,
    toasted, stemmed, and seeds removed
2 pounds (about 8 to 10 pieces) boneless chicken thighs,
    cut into 1-inch-square pieces
1 teaspoon chile powder (optional)
Salt and pepper to taste

Tacos
6 ounces asadero or Monterey jack cheese, grated
Corn tortillas

1. Roast the tomatillos on a Santa Fe Grill (see p. 39), in a very hot oven, or under a broiler until about half of the surfaces are well charred.

2. In a preheated skillet or heavy saucepan, add 1 tablespoon of oil, onions, jalapeño slices, and garlic; saute until onions are slightly browned and beginning to soften.

3. Place in a blender with roasted tomatillos, salt, sugar, herbs, vinegar, water, and dry chiles. Puree smooth.

4. In the same skillet or pan, add remaining oil and heat until just beginning to smoke (very hot). Season chicken pieces with chile powder, salt, and pepper; cook until browned on all sides.

5. Pour in sauce puree, stir well, and reduce heat to simmer. Cook, stirring occasionally, for about 10 to 12 minutes. Remove from heat. Sauce should be fairly thick.

6. Place soft corn tortillas on a baking sheet, top with chicken mixture and about a tablespoon of grated cheese. Place under a broiler or in a very hot oven (475-degree) until cheese is bubbly and starting to brown.

Serving suggestion: Try this with corn-and-black-bean salsa and oven-roasted garlic potato wedges for a delicious light supper.

SANTA FE WRAPS

Most tacos and burritos could also be called wraps, but what we are referring to here is a contemporary hybrid of a sandwich and a burrito. Wraps are wonderfully versatile. They can be made in advance, and they travel well for picnics or boxed lunches. When cut into smaller pieces, they make tasty appetizers. The following are two examples of wraps similar to ones that we developed for the newly launched "Santa fe" restaurant chain in London, England.

GRILLED VEGETABLE WRAP

Yield: 6 servings of 2 pieces each, or 4 dozen small slices for appetizers

Wrap Filling
1/8 cup olive or vegetable oil
1 tablespoon chile caribe or dry crushed red peppers, toasted
6 cloves garlic, peeled and minced
2 tablespoons chopped mixed fresh herbs (cilantro, marjoram, chives, thyme, oregano, etc.), or 1-1/2 tablespoons toasted dried Mexican oregano
2 medium zucchini squash, ends trimmed and cut lengthwise into quarter-inch-thick slices
2 medium yellow summer or crookneck squash, ends trimmed and cut lengthwise into quarter-inch-thick slices
1 Japanese eggplant, peeled and cut lengthwise into quarter-inch-thick slices
2 sweet bell peppers (red or yellow), ends cut, stemmed and seeded, membranes removed, cut into long quarters
2 poblano, New Mexican green, or Anaheim chiles, ends cut, stemmed and seeded, membranes removed, cut into long quarters
2 teaspoons coarse salt
Freshly ground black pepper
1/2 cup Chipotle Crema + extra for dipping (see p. 20)

Tacos
6 nine- to ten-inch-diameter or 8 eight-inch-diameter flour tortillas, flavored or plain

1. Mix oil, chile caribe, garlic, and herbs; let sit for at least 15 minutes to allow flavor to develop.

2. Salt and pepper sliced vegetables and place in a plastic bag or large bowl. Add oil mixture and coat vegetables evenly. Marinate for 30 minutes or overnight.

3. Cook over a charcoal or gas grill or in the oven broiler until slightly browned, cooked through but not too soft.

4. Heat tortillas one by one over a gas flame or on a comal or skillet. Spread each with 1 tablespoon of Chipotle Crema, arrange a mixture of cooked vegetables in the center, and wrap tightly to form a cylinder.

5. With a sharp knife, slice each filled tortilla in half diagonally, or slice into 8 to 10 pieces for hors d'oeuvres.

6. Serve with additional Chipotle Crema for dipping.

Note: It takes 24 to 30, 2 x 6 x 1/4-inch slices of grilled vegetables to make 6 wraps.

CHICKEN AL CARBON AND AVOCADO WRAP

Yield: 6 servings of 2 pieces each, or 4 dozen small slices for appetizers

Wrap Filling

4 boneless, skinless chicken breasts (7 to 8 ounces in size)
Juice of 1 lime
1 tablespoon vegetable oil
Salt and pepper to taste
1 tablespoon chipotle powder or other red chile powder
1/2 cup Chipotle Crema + extra for dipping
1-1/2 cups shredded romaine lettuce
1 cup Salsa Fresca (see p. 37) or other favorite salsa
2 to 3 medium-size ripe avocados, peeled, pitted, and sliced

Tacos

6 nine- to ten-inch-diameter or 8 eight-inch-diameter flour tortillas, flavored or plain

1. Sprinkle chicken breasts with lime juice, then coat with oil. Season with salt, pepper, and chile powder. Allow to sit 10 to 15 minutes.

2. Cook on a charcoal or gas grill or in the oven broiler until just cooked through, about 3 to 4 minutes per side.

3. Allow to rest for 10 minutes, then slice lengthwise in half-inch-wide strips.

4. Heat tortillas one by one over a gas flame or on a comal or skillet. Spread each with 1 tablespoon of Chipotle Crema; in the center, place some lettuce, salsa, chicken slices, and avocado; wrap tightly to form a cylinder.

5. With a sharp knife, slice each filled tortilla in half diagonally, or slice into 8 to 10 pieces for hors d'oeuvres.

6. Serve with additional Chipotle Crema for dipping.

Chipotle Crema

1-1/2 cups sour cream
3 tablespoons milk or cream
Juice of 1 lime
1/4 teaspoon salt
2 tablespoons chopped fresh cilantro
1 tablespoon or more pureed chipotle chiles in adobo to taste

1. Mix all ingredients together and chill. The crema tends to thicken over time. Thin with milk or cream as desired.

Note: We prefer the smoky-hot richness of chipotle chile here, but it can be made with other hot sauces as well.

CREAMY CHICKEN AND ALMOND TACOS

Almonds and olives are two old-world ingredients that have been embraced by cooks in Mexico. The richness of the cream balances nicely with the Mediterranean-style filling.

Yield: 18 to 20 tacos

Taco Filling

1 medium white onion, diced
4 tablespoons olive oil
1 cup diced fresh tomato or canned diced tomato
2 cloves garlic, minced
3 cups cooked and diced chicken breast
    (3 to 4 medium-size breasts)
1/4 cup sliced blanched almonds
1 tablespoon capers
2 tablespoons coarsely chopped raisins

1. Saute onion in olive oil until golden brown. Add tomatoes and cook for 3 to 4 minutes more.

2. Mix in additional ingredients, heat through, and set aside while preparing sauce.

Tacos

18 to 20 corn tortillas

1. Heat corn tortillas one at a time, place about 2 tablespoons of the warm chicken filling in each one, and roll into a cylinder.

2. Arrange tacos on a serving platter and cover with cream sauce. Garnish with chopped fresh cilantro or flat-leafed parsley.

Cream Sauce

1 small white onion, diced
4 tablespoons butter
1 poblano chile, roasted, peeled, and diced
1 green or red bell pepper, roasted, peeled, and diced
1 or 2 jalapeño chiles, stemmed, seeded, and minced
2 cups heavy or whipping cream
1 cup grated Monterey jack cheese
1/2 cup sliced pimento-stuffed green olives
Salt to taste

1. Saute onion in butter until softened. Add chiles and pepper dices; cook for an additional 3 to 4 minutes.

2. Pour in cream; bring to a boil, then reduce heat and simmer until cream is thick enough to coat the back of a spoon.

3. Stir in grated cheese and heat until completely melted. Remove from heat and mix in sliced olives. Adjust for salt.

FIRE-ROASTED CORN AND POBLANO CHILE TACOS

This dish takes its inspiration from the ubiquitous Mexican street-vendor treat *Esquites*. Made from fresh ears of sweet white corn roasted over a charcoal fire, the esquites are cut off the cob and served in a cup with chiles, lime, and crumbled cheese. When used for a taco filling, the flavors of the fresh corn and the corn tortilla contrast as well as complement each other.

Yield: 24 tacos, 8 servings

Taco Filling

6 ears fresh white or yellow corn,
    or 3-1/2 cups of frozen corn kernels may be
    substituted if fresh corn is not available
1 tablespoon butter
1/2 medium white onion, finely diced
3 cloves garlic, peeled and sliced
3 medium to large poblano chiles, roasted,
    peeled, stemmed, seeded, and diced
Dash of salt

1 teaspoon toasted dried Mexican oregano,
    or 1 teaspoon chopped fresh marjoram
3/4 cup half-and-half, or 2/3 cup heavy cream
Juice of 1 lime
6 ounces grated Monterey jack cheese
3 ounces Mexican cotija, Romano, or
    Parmesan cheese, grated

Tacos

2 tablespoons vegetable oil
Soft corn tortillas

1. Roast corn in the husk until just tender (about 10 minutes over charcoal or 18 minutes in a 425-degree oven), cool, husk, and strip.

2. Heat butter in a heavy saute or saucepan over medium-high heat. Cook onion for 1 to 2 minutes, until slightly browned on the edges. Add garlic and saute for 1 minute more.

3. Add poblano chiles, corn, salt, and oregano. Stir to combine and add half-and-half. Bring to a boil and reduce heat to simmer. Reduce liquid by half (by a third if using cream), stirring often.

4. Add lime juice and cheeses and heat through until bubbly; mixture will be fairly thick.

5. Preheat griddle, comal, or heavy skillet to medium-high heat, then brush with a light coating of oil.

6. Place tortillas a few at a time on hot surface and spoon 1-1/2 tablespoons of the mixture on top of each. When tortillas are softened, fold over to make tacos. Cook until golden brown on both sides; place in a cloth-lined basket or serving dish and cover. Repeat with remaining tacos.

Note: The filling may be made in advance and refrigerated.

Suggested accompaniments: Roasted Tomato Salsa (see Salsas, p. 34), Frijoles Charros (see p. 34), and a crispy salad.

CARNE ASADA

Carne Asada is known throughout Mexico and has become somewhat of a national dish. The most famous recipe originated in the Gulf Coast port of Tampico and was made popular by several Mexico City high-style eateries in the past century. Beef tenderloin is used in the more expensive restaurants but other cuts are commonly served at taquerias and street taco stands. Like many other traditional taco meals, the condiments and accompaniments are what make this special.

Bert's Taqueria in Santa Fe presents their tacos in an authentic Mexico City style, with various condiments and a changing selection of salsas. The owner, Fernando Olea Caballero, graciously loaned us the comal from his restaurant that we used in the photograph.

Yield: 6 to 8 servings

Taco Filling
2-1/2 pounds sirloin steak, chuck steak, or beef tenderloin
Juice of 3 limes
3 tablespoons olive or vegetable oil
1 tablespoon chipotle chile powder
1 to 2 fresh jalapeño or serrano chiles, thinly sliced
3 cloves garlic, minced
1 scallion, chopped
Freshly ground black pepper
2 teaspoons salt
8 fresh green onions (scallions), washed, trimmed, and coated with a small amount of vegetable oil

Tacos
Flour or corn tortillas

1. Trim meat of excess fat and slice or "butterfly" the meat into a sheet about 3/8-inch thick (your butcher can do this for you).

2. Place the meat between 2 sheets of plastic wrap and carefully pound it with a meat-tenderizer mallet or rolling pin to a quarter-inch thickness.

3. Coat with lime juice and brush lightly with oil. Sprinkle chile powder, jalapeño chiles, garlic, scallions, and black pepper evenly on both sides of the meat.

4. Allow to marinate for 20 to 30 minutes.

5. Salt and cook on chargrill or griddle alongside the whole green onions until beef is just cooked through and onions are beginning to brown.

6. Allow meat to rest for 5 minutes.

7. Slice the beef in long thin slices approximately a quarter-inch thick.

8. Arrange on plate, top with grilled green onions, and garnish with lime wedges.

9. Serve with warm tortillas, black beans, and/or calabacitas.

Suggested condiments: Salsa Fresca or Salsa Verde (see p. 37), toasted dried Mexican oregano, chopped fresh cilantro, Guacamole (see p. 36), sliced cucumbers and radishes, pickled or roasted jalapeño chiles, lettuce, and such crumbly cheeses as queso fresco or cotija.

STEAK AND MUSHROOM TACOS WITH GREEN CHILES

The Pink Adobe is one of Santa Fe's oldest and most popular restaurants. Chef and owner Rosalea Murphy has developed several innovative recipes that have become favorites with both locals and visitors. Her Steak Dunigan reflects the cultural fusion that has been an integral part of the city's colorful past and continues even today. Pairing the earthy flavors of mushrooms with the enticing aroma and spiciness of fire-roasted green chiles to complement the culinary icon of the West—the chargrilled steak—is nothing short of brilliant. These flavors work so well together that we have borrowed from Rosalea's original idea to create this taco recipe.

Yield: about 24 tacos

Taco Filling
2 pounds sirloin or other favorite cut of steak
5 tablespoons olive oil
4 cloves garlic, minced
2 tablespoons chopped fresh marjoram, thyme,
   or toasted dried Mexican oregano
Juice of 1 lime
Salt and freshly ground black pepper to taste

1-3/4 cups (8 ounces) sliced mushrooms (substitute
   or mix other varieties such as shiitake,
   portabello, crimini, etc.)
1 medium onion, thinly sliced
1 cup green chiles, diced, roasted, and peeled (depending
   on the season, use New Mexican, Anaheim, or
   poblano chiles; frozen green chiles also work well)
Tacos
Corn or flour tortillas

1. Marinate steak at room temperature for 30 minutes in 3 tablespoons of olive oil mixed with garlic and herbs.

2. Remove from marinade and liberally salt and pepper the steak. Cook on a chargrill or in a broiler until rare to medium rare. Allow steak to rest for 15 minutes. Cut into half-inch-wide strips and slice thinly across the strips to produce bite-size slices.

3. Place 2 tablespoons oil in a preheated skillet on medium high. When oil is very hot, add mushrooms and saute for 1 minute,

stirring several times. Add onions and continue for about 2 to 3 minutes more, until slightly browned. Cook the steak slices with mushrooms and onions for 2 to 3 minutes more, then mix in green chiles. When chiles are heated through, remove from heat and serve.

Serving suggestion: Accompany with Fresh Corn or Flour Tortillas (see p. 31), assorted condiments, cheeses, salsa, salad, and refried beans.

TACOS DE LENGUA

Noe Cano is the sous chef at the cooking school. Originally from Vera Cruz on the Gulf Coast of Mexico, Noe is appreciated by all of the instructors for his cooking skills and attention to detail. He contributed this easy-to-prepare and very tasty recipe, and even managed to convert some skeptical members of our taste panels.

In many countries, virtually every part of the animal is consumed. People are quite aware of what they are eating; in fact, many prefer these variety meats to the everyday cuts that the U.S. consumer tends to favor. Restaurants in Mexico commonly offer a variety of taco fillings that may include liver, kidneys, sweetbreads, cabeza (steer or hog's head), tripe, pig's feet, and an assortment of sausages.

Yield: 24 to 30 tacos

Taco Filling
2-1/2 to 4 pounds of calf or beef tongue
12-ounce bottle of Mexican lager
Enough water to cover the meat
2 bay leaves
1 white onion, coarsely chopped, about 3/4 cup
    (reserve half for final cooking step)
3 cloves peeled garlic

1 teaspoon whole black peppercorns
4 whole cloves
1 teaspoon salt
2 dry hot chiles (chile de arbol, pequin, or Japonese)
3 tablespoons vegetable oil or lard
Tacos
Corn tortillas

1. Place tongue in a large braising pan or pot; add beer and enough water to just cover. Bring to a boil; cook for 5 minutes, remove from heat, and skim any foam or solids that are floating on the surface.

2. Add rest of the ingredients except for reserved onion; return to a boil, then reduce heat to simmer, adding water as needed. Allow 45 minutes of cooking time per pound of meat. Completely cool tongue in the cooking liquid.

3. With a sharp knife, make an incision the length of the top side. Peel away the outer layer with your fingers or carefully with the knife. Slice 1/4- to 3/8-inch thick, then cut across and diagonally to produce square cubes.

4. Heat lard on high in a preheated skillet or saute pan. Stir-fry cubed meat with the remaining onions, a dash of salt, and freshly ground pepper. When meat is well browned serve with freshly made Corn Tortillas (see p. 31) with Salsa Verde (see p. 37) and cotija or other favorite crumbly cheese.

ROASTED WILD MUSHROOM TACOS WITH QUESO FRESCO

In the markets of Oaxaca you can see basketsful of multicolored fresh mushrooms for sale—some familiar, some not. Queso fresco is a slightly aged, crumbly, mild, farmer-style Mexican cheese. Feta or mild fresh goat cheese may be used for a stronger flavor. This recipe has been adapted from one of Zach Calkins's favorites. Zach, formerly a chef/instructor at the cooking school, has moved to the Denver area to become chef and partner in the Cadillac Ranch restaurant.

Yield: 24 soft tacos

Taco Filling
3 cloves garlic, peeled
1/4 cup olive oil
4 cups thickly sliced (about 3/8-inch thick),
    stemmed wild mushrooms (any combination
    of shiitake, chanterelle, oyster, portobello, or
    Italian brown mushrooms)

2 teaspoons fresh or dry epazote,
    or substitute toasted dried Mexican oregano
1/2 teaspoon salt
1/2 teaspoon freshly ground black pepper
3 blackened serrano chiles, stems removed and minced
8 ounces queso fresco or other mild crumbly cheese

Tacos
Soft corn tortillas

1. Puree garlic with olive oil in a blender or food processor; allow to sit for 10 minutes to infuse the flavor. Strain and discard garlic.

2. Brush mushrooms clean, then toss with infused olive oil, epazote, salt, and pepper. Spread on a cookie sheet or a cast-iron skillet; place in a preheated 425-degree oven and roast until browned and caramelized along the edges, about 8 to 10 minutes. Remove from oven.

3. Immediately toss with serrano chiles and cheese.

4. Place on heated corn tortillas, fold, and serve.

Note: Up to half of the wild mushrooms may be replaced with domestic white mushrooms to reduce the cost.

Serving suggestions: Saffron rice, Caesar salad, and your favorite salsa make these tacos perfect for a light supper, or serve them as an accompaniment to roasted meats.

POTATO, POBLANO CHILE, AND SPINACH TACOS WITH CREAM

These tasty tacos are enjoyed in classes at the cooking school. They are also featured at one of Daniel's favorite taco restaurants in Oaxaca. The filling can be made in advance and kept refrigerated for several days. Beware—even though they are very rich, many people won't be satisfied with only two.

Yield: about 5 cups of filling, enough for 20 to 24 tacos

Taco Filling
1 pound waxy boiling potatoes (about 4 to 5 red or white rose potatoes)
1 large white onion, diced
2 tablespoons vegetable oil
4 cloves garlic, peeled and sliced
2 bunches fresh spinach, washed, stems trimmed, and coarsely chopped
1 teaspoon toasted dried Mexican oregano, or 2 teaspoons chopped fresh oregano or marjoram
4 fresh poblano chiles, roasted, seeded, peeled, and cut into quarter-inch strips about 2 inches long
1 cup heavy cream, good quality sour cream, or Mexican cream
1 cup grated cheese (Monterey jack, cotija, Parmesan, fontina, or a mix)
Salt to taste

Tacos
Corn Tortillas

1. Peel potatoes and dice into 3/8-inch cubes. Cook in boiling salted water until potatoes are soft but not falling apart, about 10 to 12 minutes.

2. Heat oil in a medium-hot skillet; lightly brown onions, then add garlic and boiled potatoes and cook for 2 more minutes. Begin adding spinach a handful at a time, stirring with tongs to wilt it. When all the greens are wilted, add herbs, poblano chiles, and cream.

3. Cook on low boil, stirring occasionally, until liquid is reduced by a third; stir in cheese and continue cooking until smooth and thick. Adjust salt if needed.

4. Place in a serving dish along with a basket of warm corn tortillas so that guests may assemble their own tacos. Tomato salsas are excellent with these rich and creamy tacos.

FRESH CORN TORTILLAS

Yield: 22 to 24 three-and-a-half-inch tortillas

**2 cups dry masa harina (available from the cooking
    school and at many supermarkets)**
1/2 teaspoon salt
**1-1/3 cups (approximately) warm water
    (95 to 115 degrees)**

1. Place dry ingredients in a mixing bowl and slowly add water while stirring with a fork until dough forms a ball. Knead dough several times by hand until smooth, then form into a 2-inch-thick log. Wrap in plastic and let stand for about 30 minutes.

2. Preheat a comal, heavy skillet, or griddle to medium high (350 degrees).

3. Slice masa dough into just under 1/2-inch-thick rounds and cover to prevent drying.

4. Place a round between two sheets of plastic (a freezer bag split into 2 sheets works well) and flatten in a tortilla press to about 1/16 inch thick.

5. Peel off top sheet of plastic and gently drop tortilla from the other sheet by inverting it over the comal or griddle. Cook for about 1 minute and turn over. Cook for 30 seconds more, pushing down with a spatula several times. Cooked tortillas should have light brown speckles.

6. Keep cooked tortillas in a kitchen towel or cloth napkin to keep warm while cooking others and for serving. Serve immediately.

Note: This recipe may be prepared using a food processor. Place the dry ingredients in a bowl fitted with a steel blade. While processor is running slowly, pour the warm water through the feed and process until a smooth dough ball is formed. Proceed as above.

FRESH FLOUR TORTILLAS

Yield: 8 to 10 five-inch tortillas

2 cups all-purpose flour
1/2 teaspoon salt
1-1/2 teaspoons baking powder
3 tablespoons vegetable shortening
3/4 cup hot water (145 degrees or more)

1. Combine dry ingredients in a bowl and mix well.

2. Cut in the shortening until mix is the consistency of coarse cornmeal.

3. Add water and mix to form a soft but not too sticky dough.

4. Knead about 15 times to form a smooth dough.

5. Form into 8 to 10 equal-size balls. Cover and let stand for 20 to 30 minutes.

6. Flatten dough, rolling away from you with a small wooden dowel or rolling pin, turning dough 1/8 turn after each roll. Tortillas should be about 5 inches in diameter and of a uniform thickness.

7. Cook tortillas on a preheated 350-degree comal, griddle, or skillet for 15 to 20 seconds on the first side; flip over and cook for 20 seconds more while pressing down with a spatula. Keep warm in a cloth towel.

APPLE PIE TACOS

Dessert tacos aren't a traditional Mexican dish; however, we wanted to include one of our favorite creations. We decided on the simple approach in keeping with the easygoing and casual nature of tacos. Easy to prepare, these look like tacos and have the universally satisfying flavor of Mom's apple pie.

Yield: 8 servings

Taco Filling
4 tart apples, peeled, cored, and cut in quarter-inch-thick slices
Dash salt
1/4 cup + 2 tablespoons granulated sugar
2 tablespoons all-purpose flour
2 teaspoons cornstarch
2 tablespoons butter
2 teaspoons ground Mexican canela or cinnamon
1/2 teaspoon ground allspice
1/2 cup apple juice
Tacos
8 six-inch or 4 ten-inch flour tortillas, cut in half
2 to 3 tablespoons butter
1/8 cup powdered sugar
1 teaspoon ground Mexican canela or cinnamon

1. Preheat a heavy skillet or saucepan to medium (300 to 325 degrees).

2. Toss sliced apples with salt and 2 tablespoons of sugar, then with flour and cornstarch.

3. Place 2 tablespoons of butter in pan; when it sizzles, add apple slices.

4. Cook three to four minutes, stirring occasionally, until flour mixture combines with butter.

5. Add canela and allspice, then apple juice and 1/4 cup granulated sugar.

6. Bring to a slow boil and cook for 5 minutes, until apple slices are soft and sauce is smooth and thick. Allow to cool for a few minutes before using.

7. Spoon about 2 tablespoons of mixture on each tortilla and fold in half.

8. Melt some of the butter on a preheated comal, non-stick skillet, or griddle; place a filled tortilla in the butter. Cook about 1-1/2 minutes per side, until golden brown. Repeat for remaining tortillas. Caution: If the temperature is too high, the tortillas will brown before filling is heated through.

9. Dust tacos with powdered sugar and canela or cinnamon.

Note: These may be prepared ahead of time and re-heated in a 325-degree oven.

Serving suggestion: Accompany tacos with vanilla or cinnamon ice cream, fruit sorbet, or whipped cream.

FRIJOLES CHARROS

Yield: 8 servings

6 ounces uncooked Mexican chorizo or hot Italian sausage, casings removed, then crumbled
2 slices smoked bacon, diced
1 medium white onion, chopped
2 cloves garlic, crushed
1 teaspoon toasted dried Mexican oregano
1/2 teaspoon toasted ground cumin seed
1 ancho chile, toasted, stemmed, and seeded, then crumbled
2 bay leaves
1 teaspoon pureed chipotle chile in adobo
1/2 teaspoon salt
3-1/2 cups cooked pinto beans
1 teaspoon apple cider vinegar
1-1/2 cups chicken or pork broth

1. Cook chorizo and bacon over medium heat until fat is rendered. Pour off half the fat.

2. Continue cooking and add onion and garlic. Cook until translucent, then add oregano, cumin, ancho chile, bay leaves, and chipotle.

3. Add salt, beans, vinegar, and stock. Simmer on low for 45 minutes to 1 hour.

SPICY COLESLAW

Yield: 6 servings, enough to garnish 18 to 24 tacos

3 tablespoons apple cider vinegar
1 tablespoon vegetable oil
1/4 cup freshly squeezed lime juice
1/8 cup honey
1 teaspoon salt
1/2 cup chopped fresh cilantro
1 head red or green cabbage, shredded (about 1-1/2 pounds)
3 scallions, thinly sliced on the diagonal
2 to 3 jalapeño chiles, stemmed, seeded, and cut into very thin strips
1 large carrot, peeled and shredded

1. In a large bowl, combine liquids, salt, and cilantro with a whisk.

2. Toss with the remaining ingredients to evenly coat with the dressing.

3. Let the mixture stand at room temperature for at least 30 minutes; toss often before serving. For maximum color and flavor, serve within 3 to 4 hours.

PICKLED RED ONIONS

An excellent accompaniment for many tacos as well as for grilled and roasted meats. These onions keep for several weeks in the refrigerator.

Yield: about 3-1/2 cups

1 cup apple cider vinegar or unseasoned
    rice wine vinegar
1/2 cup water
1 clove garlic
3 tablespoons granulated sugar
6 whole allspice
3 whole cloves
8 to 10 whole black peppercorns
4 bay leaves
2 teaspoons coarse salt
2 sprigs fresh thyme or marjoram (optional)
1 habanero or serrano chile (optional)
3 large red onions, peeled and cut into eighth-inch slices
Juice of 1 orange

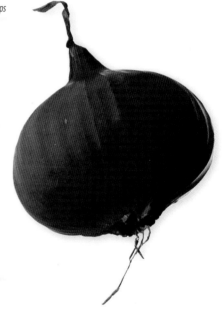

1. Place all ingredients except onions and orange juice in a non-reactive saucepan. Bring to a boil and cook for 3 minutes.

2. Put onions in a heat-proof bowl and pour hot vinegar mix over them. Add orange juice and stir well to ensure that onions are completely submerged.

3. Allow to cool at room temperature, then refrigerate.

Note: Pickled onions taste best when served at room temperature.

GUACAMOLE

Yield: 6 servings

1 medium red onion

4 medium ripe Hass avocados

1 clove garlic, minced

2 to 3 serrano or jalapeño chiles, stemmed, seeded, and minced

1/2 cup chopped fresh cilantro

1/4 teaspoon ground cumin (optional)

Salt and pepper to taste

Juice of 1/2 lime

1. Peel and cut onion in small dice. Rinse under hot water for 30 seconds, then in cold water for 30 seconds to remove the raw taste.

2. Peel and remove the pit from the avocados and place in a bowl or molcajete with all ingredients except salt, pepper, and lime.

3. Mash with hands, fork, or potato masher until avocado is fairly smooth and other ingredients have been well combined.

4. Adjust seasoning with salt and pepper.

5. Stir in lime juice when serving.

6. Garnish with Salsa Fresca (see p. 37) and/or grated, sharp aged cheese such as ricotta salata, cotija, or dry Monterey jack.

Note: Guacamole will discolor when exposed to air. Take special care when storing to ensure it is well wrapped.

SALSA FRESCA

Yield: about 3 cups

4 to 5 plum tomatoes, diced
1/2 teaspoon minced garlic
1/2 cup finely chopped red or white onion, rinsed under
    hot tap water for 30 seconds and under cold water
    for 30 more seconds, then drained
1/8 cup fresh lime juice
2 tablespoons mild vinegar such as apple cider vinegar or
    rice wine vinegar
2 or 3 fresh jalapeños, seeded and finely chopped
1/4 cup coarsely chopped cilantro
1 tablespoon olive oil (optional)
Salt to taste

1. Put tomatoes, garlic, onion, lime juice, vinegar, jalapeños, and
   cilantro in a bowl and mix well. Mixture may be coarsely pureed in
   a food processor or left intact for more texture.

2. Add olive oil, if desired, and salt to taste. Let mixture sit for
   30 minutes to allow flavors to develop.

SALSA VERDE

Yield: about 2 cups

1 dozen tomatillos, husked and rinsed under hot water
    to remove the sticky coating
6 garlic cloves, peeled
3 to 4 serrano chiles, stems removed,
    or use jalapeño chiles for a milder salsa
1 small white onion, finely chopped
Juice of 1/2 lime
1/2 teaspoon sugar
Salt to taste
1 bunch fresh cilantro

1. Boil tomatillos in enough water to cover, along with half the garlic,
   half the chiles, and half the onion for about 10 minutes. Remove
   from heat and drain; reserve cooking water. Cool. Finely mince
   remaining garlic and chiles. Coarsely chop cilantro leaves.

2. Place tomatillos, cooked onions, garlic, and chiles in a blender or
   food processor and blend, adding a little of the cooking water if
   necessary. The sauce should be thick. Pour sauce into a bowl; stir in
   reserved garlic, chiles, remaining onion, cilantro, lime juice, and
   sugar; season with salt to taste.

⊕ INGREDIENTS ⊕

Achiote Paste — A seasoning condiment prepared from the ground seeds of the tropical annatto tree, mixed with garlic, spices, and vinegar. With an almost indescribable earthy flavor, achiote is used as a seasoning for seafood, meats, and poultry.

Canela — A soft variety of cinnamon originating in Ceylon (Sri Lanka). Lightly perfumed, with a sweeter and less pungent flavor than the cinnamon commonly found in U.S. supermarkets, canela is used extensively in Mexico. Best if ground fresh, canela is usually sold in stick form. Cinnamon may be used as a substitute for canela by halving the quantity.

Cilantro — The fresh plant from the coriander seed; however it is not interchangeable with the seed in recipes. To store, re-cut the stem ends and place cut-side down in a cup or other container in shallow water. Cover with plastic and refrigerate. Widely available in most supermarkets.

Epazote — A pungent herb that grows wild in Mexico and the U.S. It is used frequently in seasoning beans, acts as an anti-flatulent, and is used as medicinal tea for stomach and digestive ailments.

Masa Harina — The dry form of *nixtamal*, the masa made from white corn that has been treated with mineral lime and then stone ground. Used for tortillas and tamales.

Mexican Oregano — A weedy-flavored herb reminiscent of, but distinctly different from, the more common Mediterranean variety. Preferred in the whole-leaf form vs. the ground form.

Tomatillo — A tart green fruit of the nightshade family used frequently in Mexican sauces. Its appearance resembles a small green tomato in papery husks. A close relative of the cape gooseberry, tomatillos are available in many supermarkets.

COOKING EQUIPMENT

Comal — A heavy flat griddle, usually made of cast iron or ceramic material, that is used for cooking tortillas and for roasting chiles, vegetables, and spices.

Santa Fe Grill — The cooking school manufactures a grill that sits over the burner of gas and electric ranges. It can be used for roasting chiles, peppers, tomatoes, and garlic.

Tortilla Press — A handy piece of equipment, usually made from cast iron or aluminum, that is used to flatten corn masa when making fresh tortillas.

TECHNIQUES: ROASTING AND TOASTING

Fresh Chiles and Bell Peppers — Fresh chiles are roasted to intensify their flavor, impart a smokiness, and facilitate removing the skin. Our favorite method is to roast over a burner with the Santa Fe Grill or over a hot fire in the charcoal grill. Chiles may also be roasted under the broiler. Arrange chiles so that they are as close to the heat source as possible and turn them several times as they begin to blister and darken to ensure even charring of the skin. When 80 to 90 percent of the skin is blistered or blackened, place in a paper or plastic bag or in a bowl covered with plastic wrap and steam for 10 to 15 minutes. Gently peel the charred skin from the chile; a few bits of remaining skin lend a rustic quality to the chile and are not a problem. You may want to wear rubber or plastic gloves to protect your hands.

Dried Whole Chiles — Arrange the chiles in a layer on a preheated (300- to 325- degree) heavy skillet or comal, or on a baking sheet in a 325-degree oven. Toast the whole chiles, turning several times, until they have softened and begun to darken around the edges (about 2 to 3 minutes). Remove from heat. When cool, remove the stem, seeds, and seed membranes; proceed as directed in the recipe.

Spices, Herbs, Seeds, and Ground Chile — Dry toasting is a method used to intensify the flavors of dry ingredients. In a dry, medium-hot, heavy skillet or comal, toast the ingredients one at a time, stirring or shaking the pan to prevent burning. When the color has begun to deepen and little wisps of smoke are forming, remove immediately and cool. Whole seeds may be ground to powder in a coffee grinder or with a mortar and pestle. Toast only what is needed for a particular recipe as most ingredients do not keep well after the application of heat.

Tomatoes and Tomatillos — To roast, arrange on a Santa Fe Grill, a hot comal, or under a broiler. Turn several times for evenness, until most of the skin has been charred. Place in a bowl to save the juices. May be pureed or chopped for sauces and salsas.

⚬ CHILES ⚬

Ancho — The dry form of the ripened, fresh poblano chile. Dark cranberry red in color with a wrinkled skin. Mild to medium heat level with sweet, dried fruit flavors reminiscent of prunes, raisins, figs, coffee, and tobacco.

Anaheim — A hybrid form of the New Mexico green chile. Milder and slightly larger, it is sometimes sold as the California green chile.

Chile de Arbol — A small, hot and flavorful, bright red chile related to the cayenne.

Chile Caribe — Crushed form of the New Mexico red chile.

Chipotle — Smoked and dried jalapeño chile. Dusty brown and ridged with a wrinkled skin, chipotle chiles have a rich, smoky, tobacco-like flavor with an intense heat.

Chipotle Chiles in Adobo — Chipotle chiles pickled in a sauce of tomatoes, vinegar, onion, garlic, and spices. Sold in whole chile form and pureed forms. Slightly less heat than the dry chipotle.

Guajillo Chile — Dried red chile pod similar to the New Mexico red chile but smaller and somewhat darker in color. Medium hot with an earthy, slightly bitter flavor.

Habanero — Extremely hot, yet full-flavored, lantern-shaped chile used extensively in the Yucatan. Ranging in color from lime green to bright orange, this chile is known for its aroma of tropical fruits and flowers as well as for its heat. The Caribbean varieties are often called Scotch bonnet peppers.

Jalapeño — Small, fresh green chile with a thick flesh. Usually fairly hot, but milder varieties are increasingly available. It is the most widely recognized hot green chile.

New Mexico Green Chile — Fresh green chiles, about 4 to 6 inches in length, with three primary varieties that range from mild to hot. Usually roasted and peeled, they are chopped for sauces and stews and stuffed for chile rellenos.

New Mexico Red Chile — The green chile has been vine-ripened until it turns red, and is then dried. These chiles have a bright, fruity flavor and are often tied together to form a decorative ristra for storage. Available as whole pods or ground into powder.

Poblano Chile — A wide-shouldered, thick-fleshed, dark green chile variety with medium to hot piquancy. Usually roasted and peeled to bring out its full flavor, the poblano is used for rellenos, sauces, and salsas.

Serrano Chile — A small, cylindrical, fresh green chile, similar to the jalapeño but smaller and thinner. Can be interchanged with the jalapeño but has a hotter flavor.

RESOURCES

Chile Today Hot Tamale
(mail order only)
2-D Great Meadow Lane
East Hanover, NJ 07936
(800) 468-7377
Web site: www.chiletoday.com
— *Dried chiles, hot sauces, and chile powders.*

Dean & Deluca
1. Catalog Department
(800) 221-7714
Web site: www.deandeluca.com
— *Dried chiles, dried posole, spices, hot sauces.*

2. 560 Broadway
New York, NY 10012
(212) 226-6800

3. 3276 M Street NW
Washington, DC 20007
(202) 342-2500

El Paso Chile Company
909 Texas Avenue
El Paso, TX 79901
(800) 274-7468
Web site: www.elpasochile.com
— *Bottled sauces, dips, pestos, etc.*

Kalustyan's
123 Lexington Avenue
    (between 28th & 29th)
New York, NY 10016
(212) 685-3451
Web site: www.kalustyans.com
— *Asian, Indian, and Mexican spices; nuts, dried fruit, grains, beans, and chile powders.*

Mo Hotta Mo Betta
(mail order only)
P.O. Box 4136
San Luis Obispo, CA 93406
(800) 462-3220
Web site: www.mohotta.com
— *Dried chiles, herbs, spices, hot sauces, and salsa.*

Pendery's, Inc.
1221 Manufacturing Street
Dallas, TX 75207
(800) 533-1870
(214) 741-1870
Web site: www.penderys.com
— *Dried chiles and spices.*

Santa Fe School of Cooking
116 West San Francisco Street
Santa Fe, NM 87501
(800) 982-4688
(505) 983-4511
(505) 983-7540 fax
Web site:
www.santafeschoolofcooking.com
— *Over twenty varieties of dried chiles and powders, huitlacoche, chipotle chiles in adobo, herbs, spices, posole, Mexican chocolate, and more.*

◎ ACKNOWLEDGMENTS ◎

A special thanks to photographer Lois Ellen Frank for use of her studio, kitchen, props, creativity, and especially for her patience. Thanks also to her assistant, Walter Whitewater, for his help in food styling.

Noe Cano, sous chef at the Santa Fe School of Cooking, was invaluable in the food-styling and recipe-testing stages. Without Noe, this book would have been more difficult and a lot less fun. Thanks to Susan Thomas and Nicole Curtis for proofreading and tasting and to all of the chefs, staff, friends, and visitors of the school for their help and feedback during the recipe testing.

We would like to express our appreciation to the following businesses and individuals for their contributions to this book: Fernando Olea Caballero of Bert's Taqueria for the use of his comal and for the wonderful taco feast he prepared; David Cohen of Old Mexico Grill for recipes, ideas, and a delicious taco lunch; and Cookworks for providing some of the textiles, dishes, and glassware for the photography. Cookworks has stores in Santa Fe, New Mexico; Bal Harbour, Florida; and Dallas, Texas. Contact Cookworks at (800) 972-3357.

∘ INDEX ∘

⚙ SANTA FE SCHOOL OF COOKING AND MARKET ⚙

The Santa Fe School of Cooking is a regional cooking school that opened its doors in December 1989. Since its opening, thousands of guests have enjoyed taking classes, participating in culinary tours, and becoming part of the school's family. The adjacent market specializes in local products and has its own product line. A mail-order catalog is also available.

If you would like to receive information about the Santa Fe School of Cooking, please copy and fill out this form, then mail to the following address:

The Santa Fe School of Cooking
116 West San Francisco Street
Santa Fe, NM 87501
(800) 982-4688 catalog information
(505) 983-4511 class information
(505) 983-7540 fax

Check out our Web site for a current class schedule, information about culinary tours, special events, or shopping on-line: *www.santafeschoolofcooking.com*

Name _____

Address _____

City _____ State _____ Zip Code _____

Phone _____